THE BEST 50

SMOOTHIES

Joanna White

BRISTOL PUBLISHING ENTERPRISES
San Leandro, California

Printed in the United Stated of America.

ISBN 1-55867-114-5

Cover design: Frank Paredes
Cover photography: John Benson
Food stylist: Suzanne Carreiro

INTRODUCTION

Smoothies are combination fruit juice drinks that have whole fruit blended in for thickness. They often include a creamy base, such as yogurt or milk. Ice or frozen fruits are generally added to chill and thicken the drink.

Because of the density, they are very filling. Often protein powders are added to make a substitute meal. Smoothies can be used as appetizers, entrées, snacks or even desserts. We now have a tremendous variety of fruits and juices available to us — so use your imagination, experiment and create to your heart's desire!

The recipes in this book generally make from 12 to 16 ounces, which is either 1 or 2 servings depending on your appetite.

HELPFUL HINTS

- Use fresh fruit juices whenever possible for maximum nutritional benefits and flavor. Be careful to read labels —

bottled juices may contain only a small amount of juice and a large quantity of sugar.

- To get more juice from fruits, make sure they are at room temperature before blending. You can also gently roll fruit (especially lemons, limes, oranges and grapefruit) back and forth on the counter to soften the pulp.

- Save the peels for garnish. A lemon stripper (or canelle knife) is a handy tool for quick garnishing.

- If the smoothie appears too thick, dilute it by adding additional ice, water or juice.

- If you prefer a thicker smoothie, increase the quantity of fruit or add more of a creamy base, such as yogurt. If you freeze the fruit ahead of time, the result will naturally be a thicker smoothie.

- To frost a glass or mug, dip it in cold water and place it in the freezer while still wet. Freeze for at least ½ hour. You can dip the rim in sugar before freezing, for effect.

- Using frozen fruit cubes is a good way to keep drinks cold without diluting them. Cut fruit (removing seeds first) into cubes, dip in lemon juice and freeze on trays. Once frozen, the fruit cubes can then be bagged and kept in the freezer for future use.

- Decorative ice cubes add a special touch. Fill an ice cube tray half full, freeze, remove tray from freezer, place a piece of fruit or decoration on top of each ice cube, cover with water and freeze solid.

- A large quantity of smoothies can be served as punch in a hollowed-out watermelon, for a decorative flare. Cut a slice close to the top, scoop out the pulp and zigzag the edges

with a sharp knife. Be sure to cut a thin slice from the bottom so that the watermelon will lie flat and not roll.

- Smoothies will separate if a creamy base has been added, so either serve immediately or plan to reblend just before serving. Also, when using sparkling water or a sparkling juice mixture, add it just before serving so that it does not lose its carbonation.

- Whenever bananas get too ripe for eating, save them for future smoothies. Remove the peel and place them in freezer bags until ready to use. Bananas generally add sweetness and thickness to smoothies.

- It is usually better to break up ice cubes before putting them into the blender. Unless you have one of the more powerful blender models that are designed to easily crush ice, it is wise to save wear and tear on your machine. Read the manufacturer's instructions for your model.

GREAT GARNISHES FOR SMOOTHIES

berries (all types, floating
on top)
candy canes
cantaloupe (balls or wedges)
chocolate (grated or curled)
cinnamon (ground or stick)
coconut (toasted or untoasted)
grapes (hung over side
of glass)
jelly beans (fun for kids!)
kiwi (slices or wedges)
lemon (slices and peels)
lime (slices and peels)
maraschino cherries

marshmallows
melon (balls or wedges)
mint leaves
nutmeg (ground or freshly
grated)
orange (slices and peels)
peppermint (candies or sticks)
pineapple (wedges or chunks,
skewered on sticks)
strawberries
whipped cream (sweetened,
unsweetened, chocolate-
flavored)

COMMON FRUITS FOR SMOOTHIES

apples
apricots
bananas
blackberries
blueberries
cantaloupes
cherries
Crenshaw melons
dates
figs
grapefruits
grapes
honeydew melons
kiwis
lemons

limes
mangoes
nectarines
oranges
papayas
peaches
pears
pineapples
plums
prunes
raspberries
strawberries
tangerines
watermelons

SWEETENERS FOR SMOOTHIES

applesauce
artificial sweeteners
bananas
barley malt
fructose
frozen fruit juice concentrates
honey

jams
maple syrup
molasses
powdered sugar
rice syrup
sugar

CREAMY BASES FOR SMOOTHIES

buttermilk
chocolate milk
cream
evaporated milk
frozen yogurt (whole, low fat
or nonfat)
goat's milk
ice cream (all flavors)

ice milk (all flavors)
milk (whole, low fat or nonfat)
rice milk (flavored or regular)
sherbet (all flavors)
soy milk (flavored or regular)
sweetened condensed milk
yogurt (whole, low fat or
nonfat)

BREAKFAST SMOOTHIES

APPLE CINNAMON DELUXE

For a change, try different spices like nutmeg or cloves. If you prefer it sweeter, add more strawberries. Garnish with a cinnamon stick.

1 cup apple juice
dash ground cinnamon
3-4 frozen strawberries
1-2 tbs. protein powder, optional
¼ cup ice cream or vanilla yogurt
3 ice cubes

Place all ingredients in a blender and process until smooth.

ORANGE PINEAPPLE DELIGHT

This is a refreshing breakfast drink. Garnish with an orange slice and a pineapple wedge.

1½ cups orange juice
½ cup canned or fresh pineapple chunks
1 frozen banana, cut into chunks
2 tbs. protein powder or ¼ cup orange yogurt
3 ice cubes

Place all ingredients in a blender and process until smooth.

STRAWBERRY CRANBERRY SLUSH

Garnish this wonderful wake-up drink with strawberries.

1½ cups cranapple juice
6 frozen strawberries
½ cup vanilla yogurt
3 ice cubes
2 tbs. protein powder

Place all ingredients in a blender and process until smooth.

BREAKFAST BLENDER SMOOTHIE

Cereals add a little crunch to your smoothie and make it "stick" with you a little longer. Garnish with a slice of banana and a strawberry.

1 frozen banana, cut into chunks
1 cup frozen strawberries
1 cup milk or strawberry yogurt
½ cup granola or sweetened corn flakes

Place all ingredients in a blender and process until smooth.

BREAKFAST BRAIN SMOOTHIE

Here is a healthy breakfast drink. The amount of orange juice concentrate or jam is based on personal preference. Rice ice cream can be found at health food stores; Rice Dream is one brand. Garnish with a slice of orange.

1 frozen banana, cut into chunks
½ cup rice milk, soy milk, buttermilk or low fat milk
½ cup orange juice
1 tbs. lecithin powder
1-2 tbs. oat bran
2-3 tbs. orange juice concentrate or low sugar jam
½ cup rice ice cream, low fat ice cream or frozen yogurt

Place all ingredients in a blender and process until smooth.

RASPBERRY ENERGIZER

This high-protein drink is great for breakfast. Soy milk and rice milk are usually found in health food stores. Garnish with a few raspberries gently placed on top.

1 pkg. (10 oz.) frozen raspberries
1 cup vanilla yogurt
2 tbs. protein powder
3 ice cubes
1 cup milk, soy milk, rice milk or juice of choice
2-4 tbs. raspberry jam, or to taste

Place all ingredients in a blender and process until smooth. Taste and determine if you want to add more jam to sweeten.

COFFEE BANANA SMOOTHIE

Occasionally cold coffee can be substituted for fruit juice in smoothies. This fits in well with the new interest in coffee drinks. Taste and adjust sweetness to your personal preference. Garnish with a slice of banana.

1 cup strong coffee, chilled
1 frozen banana, cut into chunks
½ cup cream or ice cream
powdered sugar

Place all ingredients in a blender and process until smooth.

BERRY SMOOTHIES

RED FRUIT SMOOTHIE

This smoothie has a rich flavor that will have them coming back for more. Garnish with a small bunch of grapes hanging over the side of the glass.

½ cup grape juice
1 cup cherry juice
1-2 sweet plums, chopped (peel can be left on)
2 ice cubes
2 tbs. protein powder or ¼ cup cherry yogurt, optional

Place all ingredients in a blender and process well, making sure plums are completely blended.

BLUEBERRY BLITZ

Blueberries make a dark, colorful drink. Add the frozen yogurt for a creamy texture, and if you can find blueberry yogurt, even better. Garnish with a few blueberries or a small bunch of grapes hanging over the side of the glass.

1 cup frozen blueberries
1 cup grape juice
2 ice cubes
slight pinch nutmeg
½ cup vanilla frozen yogurt, optional

Place all ingredients in a blender and process until smooth.

RED RASPBERRY RAZZLER

If you use the sugarless, fruit-sweetened jam, it really enhances the flavor. Garnish with a few raspberries gently placed on top or freeze a raspberry in an ice cube and float it on top.

1 cup frozen or fresh raspberries
$\frac{1}{2}$ cup apple or grape juice
1 cup raspberry yogurt
$\frac{1}{4}$-$\frac{1}{2}$ cup raspberry jam
$\frac{1}{2}$ cup raspberry or vanilla frozen yogurt or ice cream
2 ice cubes

Place all ingredients in a blender and process until smooth. If you wish, you can strain out the seeds before drinking.

ZESTY CRANBERRY ORANGE

Simple as can be, but oh so good. Taste and adjust sweetness by adding more cranberry sauce if necessary. Garnish with a slice of orange.

1½ cups orange juice
2 tbs. whole cranberry sauce
1 cup orange yogurt or vanilla ice cream

Place all ingredients in a blender and process until smooth.

BLACKBERRY SPRITZER

Blackberries are universally appreciated. Depending on the sweetness of the berry, you may wish to add powdered sugar. Garnish with a skewered lemon slice between two blackberries.

1 cup lemonade
1 cup fresh or canned blackberries
½ cup ginger ale
powdered sugar, optional

Place all ingredients in a blender and process until smooth. If desired, strain out the seeds before drinking.

CRANBERRY LIME FIZZ

This incredibly refreshing recipe can be expanded to make a delicious punch. Garnish with a slice of lime on the side of the glass or floating on top.

1 cup cranberry juice cocktail
½ lime, peeled, sectioned and seeded
1 cup ginger ale or 7-UP
1 cup lime sherbet
2 ice cubes

Place all ingredients in a blender and process until smooth.

SUPER STRAWBERRY SLURPEE

Sweetened condensed milk really makes a rich drink. Taste and add more condensed milk if you like it sweeter. Garnish with a whole strawberry.

1½ cups sliced strawberries
¾ cup water or strawberry soda
⅓ cup sweetened condensed milk
4-6 ice cubes

Place all ingredients in a blender and process until smooth.

TROPICAL SMOOTHIES

PINEAPPLE STRAWBERRY SUPREME

Canned pineapple chunks are used for convenience, but fresh pineapple is always preferred. Garnish with a fresh pineapple wedge and strawberries.

1 cup pineapple juice
½ cup canned pineapple chunks
½ cup sliced strawberries
1 frozen banana, cut into chunks
1-2 tbs. protein powder or ¼ cup strawberry yogurt

Place juice and pineapple in a blender and process until smooth. Add banana and protein powder; blend until smooth.

BANANA DATE DELIGHT

If you wish, play around with the spices for variety. Garnish with a fresh apple slice that has been rolled in cinnamon sugar.

1 frozen banana, cut into chunks
2-3 dates, pitted
1½ cups apple juice
½ apple, cut into chunks
dash cinnamon or nutmeg, optional

Place all ingredients in a blender and process until smooth.

PAPAYA STRAWBERRY TROPICAL

Papaya conjures up images of tropical beaches. Drink and dream! Garnish with a skewer of alternating small orange wedges and strawberries.

1 cup papaya nectar
1 cup orange juice
8 frozen strawberries
1 frozen banana, cut into chunks
$\frac{1}{4}$ cup orange or vanilla yogurt, optional

Place all ingredients in a blender and process until smooth.

PINEAPPLE PEACH PICK-ME-UP

The type of creamy base you add will totally change the flavor, so be inventive. If you use fresh peaches be sure to remove the skin first, and, depending on the sweetness, you may need to add more ice cream, sherbet or yogurt. Garnish with a pine-apple wedge or a fresh peach slice.

1 cup pineapple juice
1 cup orange juice
3/4 cup canned peach slices
1/2 cup peach ice cream, pineapple sherbet or
vanilla yogurt
4 ice cubes

Place all ingredients in a blender and process until smooth.

PAPAYA GRAPEFRUIT COOLER

This makes a great morning drink if you use protein powder or a refreshing afternoon cooler with the addition of orange sherbet.

½ cup papaya nectar
½ cup grapefruit juice
½ cup orange juice
½ cup pineapple chunks
3 ice cubes
2 tbs. protein powder or ½ cup orange
sherbet, optional

Place all ingredients in a blender and process until smooth.

PINEAPPLE APRICOT PUNCH

Apricots don't have to be peeled when using a blender. Just make sure you get the seeds out or you'll have a real mess. Garnish with a pineapple wedge or orange slice.

4-6 fresh or canned apricots
1 cup pineapple juice
½ cup orange juice
3 ice cubes
powdered sugar, optional

Place all ingredients in a blender and process until smooth.

BANANA APRICOT NECTAR

Coconut milk gives this an exotic touch. It may be a little sweet, so offset this by adding a little lemon juice. Garnish with a banana slice.

1 frozen banana, cut into chunks
1½ cups apricot nectar
½ cup coconut milk
2-3 ice cubes
few drops lemon juice, optional

Place all ingredients in a blender and process until smooth.

CITRUS SMOOTHIES

SUPER CITRUS SMOOTHIE

If you don't have mandarin oranges, you can always use fresh oranges or tangerines. Garnish with canned or fresh orange slices.

1 cup orange juice
½ cup (11 oz.) canned mandarin orange segments
½ cup grapefruit juice
2 tbs. protein powder or ¼ cup orange yogurt
3 ice cubes

Place all ingredients in a blender and process until smooth.

CITRUS PEACH POWER

If you can find peach yogurt — even better. Garnish with a wedge of grapefruit.

1 cup grapefruit juice
¾ cup fresh or canned peach slices
½ cup peach or vanilla yogurt
2-3 ice cubes

Place all ingredients in a blender and process until all peach slices are thoroughly blended.

ORANGE MANGO MADNESS

When mangoes come in season you can peel and freeze a large quantity to last year-round. Garnish with either a fresh mango slice or an orange slice.

1 cup orange juice
1 mango, cubed
3 ice cubes
½ cup orange sherbet or orange yogurt
1-2 tbs. protein powder, optional

Place all ingredients in a blender and process until fruit is totally incorporated.

ORANGE NECTARINE NECTAR

Nectarines don't really have to be peeled because the blender will grind the peel sufficiently. Taste and adjust sweetness or tartness to personal preference. Dip a slice of fresh nectarine in lemon juice to use as a garnish.

1 cup orange juice
3 nectarines, sliced
1 tbs. lemon juice
1 tbs. sugar or honey
3 ice cubes

Place all ingredients in a blender and process until smooth.

CHOCOLATE ORANGE SPARKLER

This is a famous combination that can be used like a dessert if served with a light, crispy cookie. Taste and add more frozen yogurt or ice cream if you want it "heavy on the chocolate." Garnish with a twist of orange peel.

1 cup orange juice
1 orange, peeled, sectioned and seeded
1 cup ginger ale
1 cup chocolate frozen yogurt or ice cream

Place all ingredients in a blender and process until smooth.

CITRUS RASPBERRY RIPPLE

This is a delicious and refreshing combination. Garnish with a wedge of pineapple skewered with a few raspberries.

1 cup orange juice
½ cup grapefruit juice
½ cup pineapple juice
1 cup raspberry sherbet
½ cup fresh or sweetened frozen raspberries
2 ice cubes

Place all ingredients in a blender and process until smooth. You may want to strain out the seeds before serving.

CITRUS JULIUS

This creamy and delicious smoothie is refreshing as a morning wake-up drink. Add more powdered sugar if you prefer it sweeter.

1 cup orange juice
1 grapefruit, peeled, sectioned and seeded
juice of ½ lime
2 tbs. powdered sugar
2-3 ice cubes
2 tbs. protein powder, optional

Place all ingredients in a blender and process until smooth.

PINK POWER PUNCH

Two tart fruit juices will perk you up. Taste and determine if you wish to add a little powdered sugar for sweetness. Garnish with a slice of grapefruit.

1 grapefruit, peeled, sectioned and seeded
1 cup cranapple or cranberry juice cocktail
2 ice cubes
½ cup ginger ale or sparkling water
1-2 tbs. powdered sugar, optional

Place all ingredients in a blender and process until smooth.

LEMON MINT JULEP

Here is a refreshing lemon cooler that must be garnished with a sprig of mint. Add more of the sweetener, if desired. If using honey, blend for a minute longer to thoroughly incorporate it.

1½ cups water or sparkling water
¼ cup lemon juice
½ lime, peeled, sectioned and seeded
2 tbs. finely chopped fresh mint
3-4 ice cubes
3-4 tbs. powdered sugar or honey

Place all ingredients in a blender and process until smooth.

FRUITY REFRESHER

Oranges and apples can be mixed together and enhanced with strawberry sherbet. If you can't find strawberry, use raspberry. Garnish with a twist of orange peel.

2 oranges, peeled, sectioned and seeded
2 cups apple juice
1 cup strawberry sherbet
2-3 ice cubes

Place all ingredients in a blender and process until smooth.

MELON SMOOTHIES

HONEYDEW DREAM

Honeydew melon is enhanced by a touch of honey. For garnish, consider skewering a pineapple wedge, a piece of honeydew melon and a cherry for color.

1 cup pineapple juice
1 cup honeydew melon chunks
1 tbs. honey
¼ cup pineapple sherbet or vanilla yogurt
2 ice cubes

Place all ingredients in a blender and process until smooth.

MELON MEDLEY

Try to take advantage of the exotic melons available during the summer months. Garnish with a wedge of one or both melons.

1 cup pineapple juice
½ cup chopped cantaloupe
½ cup chopped honeydew melon
2-3 ice cubes

Place all ingredients in a blender and process until smooth.

WATERMELON APPLE DREAM

Watermelon is wonderfully refreshing, especially when mixed with a creamy base. Garnish with a watermelon wedge.

1 cup chopped seeded watermelon
½ cup apple juice
½ cup chopped apple
1 cup vanilla ice cream or frozen yogurt

Place all ingredients in a blender and process until smooth.

WATERMELON ORANGE REFRESHER

An amazingly refreshing drink. Garnish with a watermelon wedge and an orange slice.

1 cup chopped seeded watermelon
1 cup orange juice
2 ice cubes
½ cup orange yogurt or orange sherbet

Place all ingredients in a blender and process until smooth.

MULTI-MELON MADNESS

This drink is also particularly satisfying as a breakfast drink.
Garnish with a skewer of all the fruits.

½ cup chopped cantaloupe
½ cup chopped seeded watermelon
½ cup chopped honeydew melon
½ cup pineapple juice
½ cup papaya nectar
2 ice cubes
2 tbs. protein powder or ¼ cup vanilla yogurt

Place all ingredients in a blender and process until fruit is completely blended.

SPARKLING WATERMELON SMOOTHIE

If you feel so inclined, try a little sparkling wine in place of the sparkling water to "warm" it up. Garnish with a watermelon wedge.

1 cup cranapple juice
1 cup chopped seeded watermelon
½ cup sparkling water or sparkling wine
2 ice cubes
½ cup vanilla ice cream or frozen yogurt

Place all ingredients in a blender and process until smooth.

CREAMY SMOOTHIES

PEACH PERFECTION

Don't be surprised at the sweetened condensed milk; it gives this drink a delightful twist — add more or less to taste. You may also want to taste before determining whether you wish to add ginger. Garnish with an orange peel.

2 peaches, peeled and seeded
¾ cup orange juice or orange-flavored sparkling water
¼ cup sweetened condensed milk
3 ice cubes
½ tsp. minced ginger root or ⅛ tsp. ground, optional

Place all ingredients except ginger in a blender and process until smooth.

ORANGE APRICOT CREAM

The banana adds natural sweetness and complements apricots well. Garnish with an orange slice.

1 cup orange juice
1 cup apricot nectar
1 frozen banana, cut into chunks
3 ice cubes
1/4-1/2 cup orange sherbet or orange yogurt

Place all ingredients in a blender and process until smooth.

PINEAPPLE PAPAYA CREAM

This is an excellent drink to help digest heavy protein meals. Both pineapple and papaya are high in digestive enzymes. Garnish with a pineapple wedge.

1 cup pineapple juice
$\frac{1}{2}$ cup papaya juice
1 frozen banana, cut into chunks
2 tbs. protein powder
$\frac{1}{2}$ cup vanilla or pineapple yogurt
3 ice cubes

Pour fruit juices in a blender and blend. Add banana. Process until smooth. Add remaining ingredients and blend until smooth.

STRAWBERRY APPLE CREAMY COCKTAIL

You can't go wrong with these two flavors. Garnish with strawberry slices or skewer the three types of fruit on a stick and serve on the side.

1 cup apple juice
$\frac{1}{2}$ cup sliced strawberries
1 frozen banana, cut into chunks
3-4 ice cubes
$\frac{1}{4}$-$\frac{1}{2}$ cup strawberry yogurt or ice cream

Place all ingredients in a blender and process until smooth.

CHERRY PINEAPPLE CREAM

This is quick and simple and is enhanced with a stemmed maraschino cherry as a garnish.

1 cup cherry juice
½ cup pineapple chunks
1 frozen banana, cut into chunks
½ cup cherry yogurt
4 ice cubes

Place all ingredients in a blender and process until smooth.

SUPER CREAMY CHERRY JUBILEE

If you use cherry-flavored yogurt or ice cream you will savor this to the last drop. Garnish with cherries — what else!

1 cup cherry juice
1 cup canned pitted cherries
4 ice cubes
1 cup frozen yogurt, ice cream or vanilla yogurt

Place all ingredients in a blender and process until smooth.

CHOCOLATE CHERRY DELIGHT

Add more chocolate syrup if you really like chocolate. Garnish with a grating of milk chocolate sprinkled on top.

1 cup cherry cider or juice
½ cup canned pitted cherries
½ cup vanilla yogurt
2 tbs. chocolate syrup
2-3 ice cubes

Place all ingredients in a blender and process until smooth.

GRAPE BERRY CREAM

This may surprise you, but a tiny amount of black pepper enhances any recipe that has strawberries in it. Be careful not to overdo it.

1½ cups grape juice
½ cup sliced strawberries
2 ice cubes
1 cup frozen strawberry yogurt or ice cream
tiniest pinch pepper

Place all ingredients in a blender and process until smooth.

CREAMY COLADA

For piña colada lovers this is a must! Garnish with an orange slice and a fresh pineapple wedge.

½ cup orange juice
½ cup crushed pineapple
⅓ cup coconut cream
1 cup milk
1 frozen banana, cut into chunks

Place all ingredients in a blender and process until smooth.

BANANA BLITZ

Banana is universally loved by all, so you can't go wrong with this one! Use a fresh banana slice as garnish.

1 frozen banana, cut into chunks
½ cup orange juice
1 cup banana ice cream or frozen yogurt
1 cup milk, rice milk or soy milk
½ tsp. banana extract

Place all ingredients in a blender and process until smooth.

APRICOT BUTTERMILK

Buttermilk gives smoothies a tangy sourness that goes well with apricots. Taste and sweeten to your personal taste — buttermilk as the creamy base usually needs a little sweetener to offset the slightly sour taste. Garnish with an apricot slice.

1 cup pineapple juice
½ cup apricot nectar
2-3 apricots, seeded
½ cup buttermilk
2-3 ice cubes
powdered sugar, optional

Place all ingredients in a blender and process until smooth.

RED GRAPE CREAM

You can change the flavor completely by using white grape juice and green seedless grapes. Taste and adjust sweetness to your personal preference. Garnish with a bunch of either color grapes hanging on the edge of the glass.

1 cup dark grape juice
1 cup red seedless grapes
½ cup buttermilk
2 tbs. powdered sugar
3 ice cubes

Place all ingredients in a blender and process for several minutes until grapes are fully blended.

TRIPLE APRICOT YOGURT YUMMY

Add more ice if you prefer to thin the drink. Add more or less jam depending on your personal taste. Garnish with a piece of apricot.

1 cup apricot nectar
1 cup chopped fresh or canned apricot
1 cup plain yogurt
4 ice cubes
¼ cup apricot jam

Place all ingredients in a blender and process until smooth.

MIXED FRUIT SMOOTHIE

This great combination refreshes and satisfies. Garnish with skewered pieces of fruit.

$\frac{1}{2}$ cup sliced strawberries
$\frac{1}{2}$ cup diced papaya
$\frac{1}{2}$ cup diced cantaloupe
1 cup orange juice
3 ice cubes
1 cup vanilla or fruit-flavored yogurt

Place all ingredients in a blender and process until smooth.

LEMON COCONUT CREAM

Lemon and coconut marry well. Play with the quantities of lemon and sherbet to reach the proper tartness or sweetness. If you wish it sweeter, add a little more lemon sherbet. Garnish with a lemon slice.

1½ cups 7-UP
½ lemon, peeled and seeded
⅓ cup coconut cream
1 cup lemon sherbet
3 ice cubes

Place all ingredients in a blender and process until smooth.

INDEX

Notes

Notes

Notes

Notes

Notes

Notes